Peter Sellers, CBE, born Richard Henry Sellers on 8th Se[illegible]ith, England, UK, was a film actor, comedian and singer. Pet[illegible]edy series The Goon Show, had several hit comic songs and [illegible] audience through his many film characterisations, inclu[illegible]e Pink Panther movie series.

Sellers made his stage debut at the Kings Theatre, Southsea, when he was 2 weeks old, having begun accompanying his parents in a variety act that toured the provincial theatres. Peter first worked as a drummer, touring England as a member of the Entertainments National Service Association (ENSA). He developed his mimicry and improvisational skills during a spell in Ralph Reader's wartime Gang Show entertainment troupe, which toured Britain and the Far East.

Sellers made his radio debut in ShowTime after the war, becoming a regular performer on BBC radio shows, including the successful radio series The Goon Show, along with Spike Milligan, Harry Secombe and Michael Bentine during the early 1950s, which ended in 1960. Peter began his movie career during the 1950s, mainly in comedies, often parodying characters of authority, including military officers and policemen, but also performed in other film genres and roles.

Sellers artistic range included the movies I'm All Right Jack (1959), Stanley Kubrick's Lolita (1962) and Dr. Strangelove (1964), What's New, Pussycat? (1965), Casino Royale (1967), The Party (1968), Being There (1979) and 5 films of the Pink Panther series (1963–78). Peter's versatility allowed him to portray a wide range of comic characters using different accents and guises, often having multiple roles within the same film, with contrasting temperaments and styles.

Satire and black humour were major features of many of his movies, with his performances having strongly influenced later comedians. Sellers was nominated 3 times for an Academy Award, twice for the Academy Award for Best Actor, for his performances in Dr. Strangelove and Being There, and once for the Academy Award for Best Live Action Short Film, for The Running Jumping & Standing Still Film (1959).

Peter won the BAFTA Award for Best Actor in a Leading Role twice, for I'm All Right Jack and for the The Pink Panther (1963), having been nominated as Best Actor 3 times. In 1980 he won the Golden Globe Award for Best Actor – Motion Picture Musical or Comedy for his role in Being There, having previously been nominated 3 times in the same category. Turner Classic Movies stated that Sellers was "one of the most accomplished comic actors of the late 20th century."

In his personal life, Peter struggled with depression and insecurities, having been an enigmatic figure, who often claimed to have no identity outside the roles that he played. His behaviour was often erratic and compulsive, having often clashed with his directors and co-stars, particularly in the mid-1970s, when his physical and mental health had deteriorated, associated with his alcohol and drug problems. Sellers was married 4 times, having had 3 children from his first 2 marriages. He died from a heart attack in 1980, aged 54. English filmmakers the Boulting brothers, described Peter as "the greatest comic genius this country has produced since Charles Chaplin."

Sellers was the son of Yorkshire-born William "Bill" Sellers (1900–62) and Agnes Doreen "Peg" (née Marks, 1892–1967), who were variety entertainers, Peg having been in the Ray Sisters troupe. Although christened Richard Henry, his parents called him Peter, after his elder stillborn brother. Peg Sellers was related to the pugilist Daniel Mendoza (1764–1836), whom Peter greatly revered, hanging an engraving of him in his office, having planned to use Mendoza's image for his production company's logo.

Sellers was just 2 weeks old when he was carried on stage by Dick Henderson, the headline act at the Kings Theatre in Southsea, the crowd having sung "For He's a Jolly Good Fellow", which caused him to cry. The family constantly toured, causing much upheaval and unhappiness in young Peter's life.

Sellers had a very close relationship with his mother, which his friend Spike Milligan later considered unhealthy for a grown man. Peter's agent, Dennis Selinger, recalled his first meeting with Peg and Peter Sellers, observing that "Sellers was an immensely shy young man, inclined to be dominated by his mother, but without resentment or objection". As an only child though, he spent much time alone.

In 1935 the Sellers family moved to North London, settling in Muswell Hill. Although Bill Sellers was Protestant, with Peg being Jewish, Peter attended the North London Roman Catholic school St. Aloysius College, run by the Brothers of Our Lady of Mercy. The family wasn't rich, but Peg insisted on an expensive private schooling for her son. Peter Evans stated that Sellers was fascinated, puzzled, and worried by religion from a young age, particularly Catholicism, while Roger Lewis believed that soon after entering Catholic school, Peter "discovered he was a Jew—he was someone on the outside of the mysteries of faith".

Sellers later observed that while his father's faith was Church of England, his mother was Jewish, "and Jews take the faith of their mother." Spike Milligan said Peter had a guilt complex about being Jewish, having recalled that Sellers was once reduced to tears when he presented him with a candlestick from a synagogue for Christmas, believing the gesture to be an anti-Jewish slur.

Peter became a top student at school, excelling at drawing, although prone to laziness, his natural talents shielding him from criticism by teachers. Sellers recalled that a teacher scolded the other boys for not studying, saying: "The Jewish boy knows his catechism better than the rest of you!"

Peter learned stagecraft by accompanying his parents on the variety show circuit, but received conflicting encouragement from them, developing mixed feelings about show business. His father doubted Sellers's abilities in entertainment, apparently once suggesting that his son's talents would only allow him to become a road sweeper, while Peter's mother consistently encouraged him.

While at St Aloysius College, Sellers began to develop his improvisational skills, having enjoyed listening to early radio comedy shows with his closest friend, Bryan Connon, who remembered that "Peter got endless pleasure imitating the people in Monday Night at Eight. He had a gift for improvising dialogue. Sketches, too. I'd be the 'straight man', the 'feed', ... I'd cue Peter and he'd do all the radio personalities and chuck in a few voices of his own invention as well."

With the outbreak of the Second World War in 1939, St Aloysius College was evacuated to Cambridgeshire but his mother didn't allow Sellers to go, so his formal education ended at the age of 14. The family moved to the north Devon town of Ilfracombe, early in 1940, where Peter's maternal uncle managed the Victoria Palace Theatre, where he got his first job, aged 15, starting as a caretaker.

Sellers was steadily promoted, becoming a box office clerk, usher, assistant stage manager and lighting operator, also having been offered some small acting parts. Working backstage gave him a chance to study actors including Paul Scofield. Peter became close friends with Derek Altman, with whom he launched his first stage act, under the name "Altman and Sellers", playing ukuleles, singing, and telling jokes.

During his backstage theatre job, Peter began practising on a set of drums that belonged to the band Joe Daniels and his Hot Shots, Daniels having noticed his efforts then given him practical instructions. The drums well-suited Sellers's temperament and artistic skills, Spike

Milligan later observing that Peter was very proficient on the drums, so might have remained a jazz drummer, had he lacked his skills in mimicry and improvisation.

As the war progressed, Sellers continued to develop his drumming skills, having played with a series of touring groups, including those of Oscar Rabin, Henry Hall and Waldini, as well as his father's quartet, before he left to join a band from Blackpool. Peter became a member of the Entertainments National Service Association (ENSA), which provided entertainment for British forces and factory workers during the war. Sellers also performed comedy routines at these concerts, including impersonations of George Formby, with Peter accompanying his own singing on ukulele.

In September 1943, he joined the Royal Air Force, although it is unclear whether he volunteered or was conscripted, his mother having unsuccessfully tried to have him deferred on medical grounds. Sellers wanted to become a pilot, but his eyesight restricted him to ground staff duties, which he found dull, so he auditioned for Squadron Leader Ralph Reader's RAF Gang Show entertainment troupe, was accepted then toured the UK, before the troupe was transferred to India.

Peter's tour also included Ceylon and Burma, although the duration of his stay in Asia is unknown, before he served in Germany and France after the war. David Lodge, who became friends with Sellers, said he was "one of the best performers ever" on the drums, having developed a great ability to impersonate military officers during this period.

In 1946, Peter performed in his final show with ENSA, starring in the pantomime Jack and the Beanstalk, at the Théâtre Marigny in Paris, before being posted back to England shortly afterwards to work at the Air Ministry then being demobilised later that year. On resuming his theatrical career, Sellers was only able to get sporadic work, having been fired after one performance of a comedy routine in Peterborough. However, the headline act, Welsh vocalist Dorothy Squires, persuaded the management to reinstate him.

Peter also continued his drumming, having been billed on his appearance at The Hippodrome in Aldershot as "Britain's answer to Gene Krupa". In March 1948 Sellers had a 6-week run at the Windmill Theatre in London, which mainly staged revue acts, Peter providing the comedy turns in between the nude shows.

Sellers wrote to the BBC in 1948 then following an audition he made his TV debut in New To You, on 18 March 1948, with his act, largely based on impressions, being well received, so he returned the following week. However, frustrated with the slow pace of his career, Peter telephoned BBC radio producer Roy Speer, pretending to be Kenneth Horne, star of the radio show Much-Binding-in-the-Marsh.

Speer called Sellers a "cheeky young sod" for his efforts, but gave him an audition, which led to his brief appearance on 1st July 1948 on ShowTime then to work on Ray's a Laugh with comedian Ted Ray. By October 1948, Peter was a regular radio performer, appearing in Starlight Hour, The Gang Show, Henry Hall's Guest Night and It's Fine To Be Young.

The BBC Third Programme began to broadcast the comedy series Third Division, towards the end of 1948, which starred Harry Secombe, Michael Bentine and Sellers among others. One evening, Peter and Bentine visited the Hackney Empire, where Secombe was performing, with Bentine introducing Sellers to Spike Milligan. The 4 would meet up at Grafton's public house near Victoria, owned by Jimmy Grafton, who was also a BBC script writer. The 4 comedians dubbed him KOGVOS, Keeper of Goons and Voice of Sanity, with Grafton later editing some of the first Goon Shows.

In 1949, Peter started dating Anne Howe, an Australian actress who lived in London. Sellers proposed to her in April 1950 then the couple were married in London, on 15 September 1951. Their son, Michael, was born on 2nd April 1954 then their daughter, Sarah, followed in 1958.

Sellers's introduction to film work came in 1950, where he dubbed the voice of Alfonso Bedoya in The Black Rose, while continuing to work with Bentine, Milligan, and Secombe. On 3rd February 1951, Peter made a demo tape titled The Goons then sent it to the BBC producer Pat Dixon, who accepted it. The first Goon Show was broadcast on 28th May 1951, when against their wishes, they appeared under the name Crazy People. Sellers appeared in The Goons until the last programme of the 10-series run, broadcast on 28 January 1960. Peter played 4 main characters—Major Bloodnok, Hercules Grytpype-Thynne, Bluebottle and Henry Crun—with 17 minor ones.

Having begun with 370,000 listeners, the show peaked at 7 million in Britain, being described by one newspaper as "probably the most influential comedy show of all time". The BBC stated that it had the effect of launching Sellers career "on the road to stardom". In 1951 the Goons feature film debut was Penny Points to Paradise.

Peter then wrote the script to Let's Go Crazy with Spike Milligan, the earliest movie to showcase Sellers's ability to portray a series of different characters within the same film, before he again appeared opposite his Goons co-stars, in the 1952 flop, Down Among the Z Men. In 1954, Peter was cast opposite Sid James, Tony Hancock, Raymond Huntley, Donald Pleasence and Eric Sykes in the British Lion Film Corporation comedy production, Orders Are Orders. John Grierson believed that this was Sellers's breakthrough role on screen, crediting the movie with launching the film careers of both Peter and Hancock.

Sellers then took a number of small roles, including that of a police inspector in John and Julie (1955), before getting a larger part in the 1955 Alexander Mackendrick-directed Ealing comedy The Ladykillers, in which he starred opposite Alec Guinness, Herbert Lom and Cecil Parker as Harry Robinson, the Teddy Boy. Peter Evans thought that this was Peter's first good role, The Ladykillers being successful both in Britain and the US, with the movie being nominated for an Academy Award for Best Original Screenplay.

The following year Sellers appeared in 4 more TV series based on The Goons, which aired on Britain's new ITV channel: The Idiot Weekly, Price 2d, A Show Called Fred and Son of Fred. In 1957 film producer Michael Relph, impressed with Peter's portrayal of an elderly character in Idiot Weekly, cast the 32-year-old actor as a 68-year-old projectionist, in Basil Dearden's The Smallest Show on Earth, supporting Bill Travers, Virginia McKenna and Margaret Rutherford.

The film was a commercial success, becoming regarded as a minor classic of British screen comedy in the post-war era, Sellers then playing the growling voice of Winston Churchill, in the BAFTA award winning movie, The Man Who Never Was. Later in 1957 Peter portrayed a TV star with a talent for disguises, in Mario Zampi's offbeat black comedy The Naked Truth, opposite Terry-Thomas, Peggy Mount, Shirley Eaton and Dennis Price.

Increasing problems in Sellers personal life, led him into having periodic consultations with astrologer Maurice Woodruff, who held considerable sway over his later career. After a chance meeting with a North American Indian spirit guide in the 1950s, Peter became convinced that he was haunted by the music hall comedian Dan Leno, who died in 1904, believing that he guided his career and life-decisions. Sellers was a member of the Grand Order of Water Rats, the exclusive theatrical fraternity founded by Leno in 1890.

In 1958 Peter starred with David Tomlinson, Wilfrid Hyde-White, David Lodge and Lionel Jeffries as a chief petty officer, in Val Guest's, Up the Creek. Guest later stated that he'd written and directed the film as a vehicle for Sellers, thus having started Peter's movie career. To practice his voice, Sellers purchased a reel-to-reel tape recorder.

The film received critical acclaim in the US, Roger Lewis having regarded it as an important practice ground for Peter, who then featured with Terry-Thomas, as one of a pair of comic villains in George Pal's, Tom Thumb (1958), a musical fantasy movie, opposite Russ Tamblyn, Jessie Matthews and Peter Butterworth. Terry-Thomas later said that "my part was perfect, but Peter's was bloody awful. He wasn't difficult about it, but he knew it". However, his performance was a major landmark in Sellers's career, being his first contact with the Hollywood film industry.

Peter released his first studio album in 1958, titled The Best of Sellers; a collection of sketches and comic songs, which were performed as a variety of comic characters. Produced by George Martin then released on Parlophone, the L.P. reached # 3 on the UK Albums Chart. That same year, Peter made his first movie with John and Roy Boulting, with Carlton-Browne of the F.O., a comedy in which he played a supporting role for the film's lead, Terry-Thomas.

Before the release of the movie, the Boultings, along with Sellers and Thomas in the cast, started filming I'm All Right Jack, which became the highest grossing film at the British box office in 1960. In preparation for his role as Fred Kite, Peter watched footage of union officials. The role earned him a BAFTA, with The Manchester Guardian's critic having regarded it as Sellers's best screen performance to date.

In between Carlton-Browne of the F.O. and I'm All Right Jack, Peter starred in The Mouse That Roared, a movie in which Jean Seberg also appeared, directed by Jack Arnold. He played 3 leading and distinct roles: the elderly Grand Duchess, the ambitious Prime Minister and the innocent and clumsy farm boy, selected to lead an invasion of the United States. The film received universally high praise from critics.

After the completion of I'm All Right Jack, Sellers recorded a new series of The Goon Show. Over the course of 2 weekends, he took his 16mm cine-camera to Totteridge Lane in London to film himself, Spike Milligan, Mario Fabrizi, Leo McKern and Richard Lester. Originally intended as a private movie, the 11-minute long Running Jumping & Standing Still Film was screened at the 1959 Edinburgh and San Francisco film festivals.

It won the award for best fiction short in the latter festival, and received an Academy Award nomination for Best Short Subject (Live Action). In 1959 Peter released his second L.P., Songs For Swinging Sellers, which also reached # 3 in the UK Albums Chart. Peter's last movie of the fifties was The Battle of the Sexes, a comedy directed by Charles Crichton.

In 1960 Sellers portrayed an Indian doctor, Dr Ahmed el Kabir, in Anthony Asquith's romantic comedy The Millionairess, a film based on the George Bernard Shaw play of the same name. Peter wasn't interested in the role, until he learned that Sophia Loren was to be his co-star. When asked about Loren, he said to reporters "I don't normally act with romantic, glamorous women ... she's a lot different from Harry Secombe."

Sellers and Loren developed a close relationship during filming, culminating in Peter declaring his love for her in front of his wife. Sellers also woke his son at night to ask: "Do you think I should divorce your mummy?" Roger Lewis observed that Peter immersed himself completely in his characters during productions, saying that "he'd play a role as an Indian doctor, and for the next 6 months, he'd be an Indian in his real life."

The movie inspired the George Martin-produced novelty hit single "Goodness Gracious Me", with Sellers and Loren, which reached # 4 on the UK Singles Chart in November 1960. A follow-up single by the duo, Bangers and Mash, reached # 22 on the UK chart. The songs were included on an L.P. released by the pair, Peter & Sophia, which reached # 5 on the UK Albums Chart.

In 1961 Sellers made his directorial debut with Mr. Topaze, in which he also starred, the film being based on the Marcel Pagnol play Topaze. Peter portrayed an ex-schoolmaster in a small French town, who turned to a life of crime. The movie and Sellers's directorial abilities got an unenthusiastic response from the public and critics alike, Peter rarely having referred to it again.

The same year Sellers starred in the Sidney Gilliat-directed Only Two Can Play, a film based on the novel That Uncertain Feeling by Kingsley Amis. He was nominated for the Best British Actor award at the 16th British Academy Film Awards for his role as John Lewis, a frustrated Welsh librarian, whose affections swung between the glamorous Liz (Mai Zetterling), and his long-suffering wife Jean (Virginia Maskell).

In 1962 Peter played a retired British army general, in John Guillermin's Waltz of the Toreadors, based on the play of the same name. The movie was widely criticised for its slapstick cinematic adaption, with director Guillermin himself having regarded the film an "amateurish" effort. However, Sellers won the San Sebastián International Film Festival Award for Best Actor and a BAFTA award nomination for his performance, which was well received by the critics.

Stanley Kubrick asked Peter to play the role of Clare Quilty in the 1962 movie Lolita, opposite James Mason and Shelley Winters. Kubrick had seen Sellers in The Battle of the Sexes and listened to the album The Best of Sellers, having been impressed by the range of characters he could portray.

Peter was apprehensive about accepting the role, doubting his ability to successfully portray the part of a flamboyant American TV playwright, who Sellers regarded as "a fantastic nightmare, part homosexual, part drug addict, part sadist". Stanley encouraged Peter to improvise, having stated that he would often reach a "state of comic ecstasy".

Kubrick had American jazz producer Norman Granz record parts of the script for Sellers to listen to, so he could study the voice and develop confidence, giving Sellers a free artistic licence. Peter later stated that his relationship with Stanley became one of the most rewarding of his career.

Writing in The Sunday Times, Dilys Powell observed that Sellers gave "a firework performance, funny, malicious, only once for a few seconds overreaching itself, and in the murder scene, which is both prologue and epilogue, achieving the macabre in comedy". Towards the end of 1962, Peter appeared in The Dock Brief, a legal satire directed by James Hill, co-starring Richard Attenborough.

His son Michael stated that in1962 Sellers asked him and his sister Sarah "who we love more, our mother or him. Sarah, to keep the peace, said, 'I love you both equally'. I said, 'No, I love my mum.'" This prompted Peter to throw both children out, saying that he never wanted to see them again then at the end of that year his marriage to Anne broke down. In 1963, Sellers starred as gang leader "Pearly Gates" in Cliff Owen's The Wrong Arm of the Law, which was followed by his portrayal of a vicar, in Heavens Above!

"I'll play Clouseau with great dignity, because he thinks of himself as one of the world's best detectives. Even when he comes a cropper, he must pick himself up with that notion intact. The original script makes him out to be a complete idiot. I think a forgivable vanity would humanize him and make him kind of touching. It's as if filmgoers are kept one fall ahead of him."

—Sellers on portraying Clouseau.

After his father's death in October 1962, Peter decided to leave England then was approached by director Blake Edwards, who offered him the role of Inspector Clouseau in The Pink Panther, after Peter Ustinov had backed out of the movie. Edwards later recalled his feelings as "desperately unhappy and ready to kill, but as fate would have it, I got Mr. Sellers instead of Mr. Ustinov—thank God!"

Peter accepted a fee of £90,000 for 5 weeks' work on location in Rome and Cortina. The film starred David Niven in the principal role, with two other actors—Capucine and Claudia Cardinale—having more prominent roles than Sellers. However, Peter Evans stated that Peter's performance was regarded as being on par with that of Charlie Chaplin and Buster Keaton. Although the Clouseau character was in the script, Sellers created the personality, devising the costume, accent, make-up, moustache and trench coat.

The Pink Panther was released in the UK in January 1964, receiving a mixed reception from the critics, although Penelope Gilliatt, writing in The Observer, said that Sellers had a "flawless sense of mistiming" in a performance that was "one of the most delicate studies in accident-proneness since the silents".

Despite the views of the critics, the movie was one of the top ten grossing films of the year. Peter was nominated for the Golden Globe Award for Best Actor – Motion Picture Musical or Comedy at the 22nd Golden Globe Awards, and for a Best British Actor award at the 18th British Academy Film Awards.

In 1963, Stanley Kubrick cast Sellers to appear in Dr. Strangelove or: How I Learned to Stop Worrying and Love the Bomb, alongside George C. Scott, Sterling Hayden, Keenan Wynn and Slim Pickens. Peter and Stanley got on famously during the movie's production, having had the greatest of respect for each other, sharing a keen interest in photography.

The director asked Sellers to play 3 roles: US President Merkin Muffley, Dr. Strangelove and Group Captain Lionel Mandrake of the RAF. Peter was initially hesitant about taking on these diverse characters, but Kubrick prevailed. Some accounts state that Sellers was also invited to play the part of General Buck Turgidson, but turned it down because it was too physically demanding.

Stanley later commented that the idea of having Peter play so many of the film's key roles was that "everywhere you turn there is some version of Peter Sellers holding the fate of the world in his hands". Sellers was especially anxious about successfully playing the role of Kong and accurately affecting a Texan accent.

Kubrick requested screenwriter Terry Southern to record a tape of Kong's lines in his natural accent, so Peter could get sufficient control of the accent after practising with it, before starting shooting scenes in the aeroplane. After the first day's filming, Sellers sprained his ankle while leaving a restaurant, being unable to work in the cramped cockpit set, so Kubrick then re-cast Slim Pickens as Kong.

The 3 parts Peter played were distinct, "variegated, complex and refined", critic Alexander Walker believing that the roles "showed his genius at full stretch". Sellers played Muffley as a bland, placid intellectual, in the mould of Adlai Stevenson, while he portrayed Mandrake as an unflappable Englishman and Dr. Strangelove, a character influenced by pre-war German cinema, as a wheelchair-bound fanatic.

The Times critic wrote that the movie included, "three remarkable performances from Mr. Peter Sellers, masterly as the President, diverting as a revue-sketch ex-Nazi US Scientist ... and acceptable as an RAF officer, although the critic from The Guardian thought his portrayal of the RAF officer alone was, "worth the price of an admission ticket". Peter was nominated for an Academy Award for Best Actor at the 37th Academy Awards for his performance in all 3 roles, and the Best British Actor award at the 18th British Academy Film Awards.

Between November 1963 and February 1964, Sellers began filming A Shot in the Dark, an adaptation of a French play, L'Idiote by Marcel Achard. Peter found both the part and the director, Anatole Litvak, uninspiring, so the producers brought in Blake Edwards to replace Litvak. Together with writer William Peter Blatty, they turned the script into a Clouseau comedy, adding Herbert Lom as Commissioner Dreyfus and Burt Kwouk as Cato.

During filming, Sellers's relationship with Edwards became strained, the two often stopping speaking to each other during filming, communicating only by the passing of notes. Peter's personality was described by others as difficult and demanding, often clashing with fellow actors and directors. Upon its release in late June 1964, Bosley Crowther observed the "joyously free and facile way," in which Sellers had developed his comedy technique.

"I feel extremely vulnerable, and I need help a lot. A lot. I suppose I feel mainly I need the help of a woman. I'm continually searching for this woman. They mother you, they're great in bed, they're like a sister, they're there when you want to see them, they're not there when you don't. I don't know where they are. Maybe they're around somewhere. I'll find one, one of these days."

—Sellers on his need for women.

Towards the end of filming, in early February 1964, Peter met Britt Ekland, a Swedish actress who'd arrived in London to film Guns at Batasi. On 19 February 1964, just ten days after their first meeting, the couple married. Sellers soon showed signs of insecurity and paranoia, sometimes becoming highly anxious and jealous, as when Ekland starred opposite attractive men.

Shortly after the wedding, Peter started filming on location in Twentynine Palms, California for Billy Wilder's Kiss Me, Stupid, opposite Dean Martin and Kim Novak. The relationship between Wilder and Sellers became strained, the two having had very different approaches to work, so often clashed.

On the night of 5 April 1964, prior to making love with Ekland, Peter inhaled amyl nitrites (poppers), as a sexual stimulant in his search for "the ultimate orgasm", having then suffered a series of 8 heart attacks in 3 hours. His condition forced him to withdraw from the filming of Kiss Me, Stupid, being replaced by Ray Walston. Wilder was unsympathetic about the heart attacks, saying "you have to have a heart before you can have an attack".

After spending time recuperating, Sellers returned to filming in October 1964, playing King of the Individualists, alongside Ekland, in A Carol for Another Christmas, a feature-length United Nations special, broadcast in the US on the ABC channel, on 28 December 1964. Peter had been concerned that his heart attacks might have caused brain damage, so he'd be unable to remember his lines, but he was reassured that his memory and abilities were unimpaired after filming.

Sellers then played the role of the perverted Austrian psychoanalyst Doctor Fritz Fassbender, in Clive Donner's What's New Pussycat?, appearing alongside Peter O'Toole, Romy Schneider, Capucine, Paula Prentiss and Ursula Andress. The movie was the first screenwriting and acting credit for Woody Allen, having featured Sellers in a love triangle. Because of Peter's poor health, his insurance cost producer Charles K. Feldman $360,000.

Sellers became a close friend of Antony Armstrong-Jones, 1st Earl of Snowdon, a photographer who was then married to Princess Margaret. Snowdon shared the love of women, photography, fine wine and fast cars with Peter, both also being prone to bouts of depression. They spent many weekends together with their wives, having also taken several holidays together in Sardinia, on board Sellers's yacht Bobo.

On 20 January 1965, Sellers and Ekland announced the birth of a daughter, Victoria. They moved to Rome in May to film, After the Fox, an Anglo-Italian production, in which they both appeared. The movie was directed by Vittorio De Sica, whose English Peter struggled to understand, having tried to get De Sica fired, causing tensions on the set. Sellers also became unhappy with his wife's performance, triggering arguments, during one of which Peter threw a chair at Ekland. However, despite these conflicts, the script was praised for its wit.

Following the success of What's New Pussycat?, Charles Feldman brought together Sellers and Woody Allen again for his next project, Casino Royale, which also starred Orson Welles, with Peter signing a $1 million contract for the movie. Seven screenwriters worked on the project, with filming having been chaotic, Ekland stating that Sellers was "so insecure, he won't trust anyone".

A poor working relationship soon developed between Sellers and Welles, with Peter demanding that the two shouldn't share the same set then leaving the movie before his part was complete. A further agent's part was then written for Terence Cooper, to cover Sellers's departure.

Shortly after leaving Casino Royale, Peter was appointed a Commander of the Most Excellent Order of the British Empire (CBE) in honour of his career achievements. The day before his investiture at Buckingham Palace, Sellers and Ekland argued, with Britt scratching his face, so Peter had a make-up artist cover the marks. Ekland later said that although they argued, Sellers never hit her.

During his next film, The Bobo, which again co-starred Britt, the couple's marital problems worsened. Three weeks into production in Italy, Peter told director Robert Parrish to fire his wife, saying "I'm not coming back after lunch if that bitch is on the set". Ekland later stated that their marriage was "an atrocious sham" by this stage.

In the midst of filming The Bobo, Sellers's mother had a heart attack, Parrish having asked Peter if he wanted to visit her in hospital, but Sellers remained on set. She died within days, without Peter having seen her, being deeply affected by her death and remorseful at not having returned to London to see her. Ekland served him with divorce papers shortly afterwards. The divorce was finalised on 18 December 1968, with Sellers's friend Spike

Milligan having sent Britt a congratulatory telegram. Upon its release during September 1967, The Bobo was poorly received.

Peter's first movie appearance of 1968 was a reunion with Blake Edwards, for the fish-out-of-water comedy The Party, in which he starred alongside Claudine Longet and Denny Miller. He played Hrundi V. Bakshi, a bungling Indian actor, who accidentally received an invitation to a lavish Hollywood dinner party. Peter Evans, considered the character as "clearly an amalgam of Clouseau and the doctor in The Millionairess".

Roger Lewis observed that like a number of Sellers's characters, Bakshi was played in a sympathetic and dignified manner. Later that year he returned in Hy Averback's, I Love You, Alice B. Toklas, playing an attorney who abandoned his lifestyle to become a hippie. Roger Ebert of the Chicago Sun-Times gave the film 3 stars, saying that Peter was "back doing what he does best", although he also said that in Sellers's latest movies he'd "been at his worst recently".

In 1969 Peter starred opposite Ringo Starr in the Joseph McGrath-directed film The Magic Christian, portraying Sir Guy Grand, an eccentric billionaire who played elaborate practical jokes on people. The critic Irv Slifkin considered the movie to have been a reflection of the cynicism of Sellers, describing the film as a "proto-Pythonesque adaption of Terry Southern's semi-free-form short novel", and "one of the strangest films to be shown at a gala premiere for Britain's royal family". The movie, a satire on human nature, was generally viewed negatively by critics. Roger Greenspun of The New York Times regarded the film as being of variable quality, having summarised it as a "brutal satire".

A cameo appearance in A Day at the Beach (1970), was followed by a serious role later in 1970, as an ageing businessman who seduced Sinéad Cusack, in Hoffman then Peter starred in Roy Boulting's, There's a Girl in My Soup, opposite Goldie Hawn. The movie was a major commercial success, becoming the 7th most popular film at the British box office in 1970.

Andrew Spicer, writing for the British Film Institute's Screenonline, believed that although Sellers preferred playing romantic roles, he "was always more successful in parts that sent up his own vanities and pretensions, as with the TV presenter and narcissistic lothario he played in There's a Girl in My Soup". The movie was seen as a slight upturn his career but Peter's next films, including Rodney Amateau's Where Does It Hurt? (1972) and Peter Medak's Ghost in the Noonday Sun (1974), were again poorly received, with his acting having been viewed as frenetic rather than funny.

Despite these setbacks, Sellers won the Best Actor award at the 1973 Tehran Film Festival, for his tragi-comedic role as a street performer, in Anthony Simmons's The Optimists of Nine Elms. Fellow comedian and friend Spike Milligan, believed that the early 1970s were for Peter "a period of indifference, and it would appear at one time that his career might have come to a conclusion".

This was echoed by Evans, who observed that out of 9 movies during the period, 3 were never released, with 5 having flopped, only There's a Girl in My Soup being a success. In his private life, he'd been seeing the 23-year-old model Miranda Quarry, the couple getting on 24 August 1970, despite Sellers's doubts about his decision to re-marry, expressed to his agent, Dennis Selinger.

On 20 April 1972, Peter reunited with Milligan and Harry Secombe, to record The Last Goon Show of All, which was broadcast on 5th October. In May 1973, with his third marriage failing, Sellers went to the theatre to watch Liza Minnel i perform, becoming entranced with Minnelli. The pair got engaged 3 days later, despite Minnelli's betrothal to Desi Arnaz, Jr., and Sellers still being married but their relationship only lasted a month before breaking up.

Peter's friends were concerned that he was having a nervous breakdown by 1974. Directors John and Roy Boulting regarded Sellers as "a deeply troubled man, distrustful, self-absorbed, ultimately self-destructive. He was the complete contradiction." Peter was shy and insecure when out of character. When he was invited to appear on Michael Parkinson's eponymous chat show in 1974, he withdrew the day before, saying to Parkinson 'I just can't walk on as myself".

When he was told he could come on as someone else, he appeared dressed as a member of the Gestapo. After a few lines in keeping with his assumed character, he stepped out of the role then settled down, Parkinson saying that he, "was brilliant, giving the audience an astonishing display of his virtuosity". In 1974, Sellers again said that he'd communicated with the long-dead music hall comic Dan Leno, who'd advised him to return to the role of Clouseau.

That year Peter portrayed a "sexually voracious" Queen Victoria, in Joseph McGrath's comedic biographical film of the Scottish poet William McGonagall, The Great McGonagall, starring opposite Milligan and Julia Foster. However, the movie was a critical failure, with Sellers's career and life having reached an all-time low, having agreed to accept salaries of £100,000 with 10% of the gross to appear in TV productions and ads, well below the £1 million he'd once commanded / film.

In 1973, Peter appeared in a Benson & Hedges cinema commercial then in 1975, he appeared in a series of ads for Trans World Airlines, in which he played several eccentric characters, including Thrifty McTravel, Jeremy "Piggy" Peak Thyme and an Italian singer, Vito. Michael Starr asserted that Sellers showed enthusiasm for these roles, although the airline campaign failed commercially.

A turning point in Peter's career came in 1974, when he teamed up with Blake Edwards to make The Return of the Pink Panther, starring alongside Christopher Plummer, Herbert Lom and Catherine Schell. The film was shot on a budget of £3 million, having earned $33 million at the box office following its release in May 1975, reinvigorating Sellers's career as an A-list moviestar.

Peter received a nomination for the Best Actor – Musical or Comedy award for his performance at the 33rd Golden Globe Awards then he followed it with The Pink Panther Strikes Again. During filming from February to June 1976, the already fraught relationship between Sellers and Blake Edwards seriously deteriorated.

Edwards said of Peter's mental state at the time of The Pink Panther Strikes Again, "If you went to an asylum and you described the first inmate you saw, that's what Peter had become. He was certifiable." In declining physical health, Sellers was unbearable on set at times, his behaviour being regarded as unprofessional and childish, frequently having thrown tantrums, often threatening to abandon projects.

Peter Evans stated that Sellers was a "volatile and perplexing character, who left a trail of misery in his private life", saying that Sellers had a "compulsive personality and was an eccentric hypochondriac," who became addicted to various medicines on top of his recreational drug habits during the period.

His difficult behaviour during productions was widely reported, having made it harder for Peter to get employment in the industry, at a time when he most needed the work. Despite Sellers's deep personal problems, The Pink Panther Strikes Again was well received critically. Vincent Canby of The New York Times said of Peter in the movie:

"There is, too, something most winningly seedy about Mr. Sellers' Clouseau, a fellow who, when he attempts to tear off his clothes in the heat of passion, gets tangled up in his necktie and who, when he masquerades—for reasons never gone into—as Quasimodo, overinflates his hump with helium." Peter received a further nomination at the 34th Golden Globe Awards for his performance.

"'He causes pain to everyone who gets close to him ... Even when you're the victim of his outrageous behaviour, his selfishness, or one of his tantrums, you always found yourself smiling about it afterwards, even if you had to do it through gritted tears".

—Spike Milligan on Peter Sellers.

In March 1976 Sellers began dating actress Lynne Frederick, whom he married on 18 February 1977. Roger Lewis stated that of all of Peter's wives, Frederick was the most poorly treated, Julian Upton having likened it to a boxing match between a heavyweight and a featherweight, a relationship that "oscillated from ardour to hatred, reconciliation and remorse."

Peter Evans stated that Spike Milligan detested his friend's choice of partner, believing she was to blame for his increasing alcohol and cocaine dependency. On 20 March 1977, Sellers suffered a second major heart attack during a flight from Paris to London, following which he was fitted with a pacemaker.

Peter returned from his illness to star in Revenge of the Pink Panther, which was a commercial success, but the critics were tiring of Inspector Clouseau. Julian Upton believed that the strain behind the scenes had begun to manifest itself in the sluggish pace of the film, describing it as a "laboured, stunt-heavy hotchpotch of half-baked ideas and rehashed gags".

Sellers had also become tired of the role, saying after production, "I've honestly had enough of Clouseau—I've got nothing more to give". Steven Bach, the senior vice-president and head of worldwide productions for United Artists, who worked with Peter on Revenge of the Pink Panther, regarded Sellers as "deeply unbalanced, if not committable: that was the source of his genius and his truly quite terrifying aspects as manipulator and hysteric."

Peter refused to seek professional help for his mental issues, saying that he'd no personality, being almost unnoticeable, which meant that he "needed a strongly defined character to play." When he appeared on The Muppet Show in 1978, a guest appearance for which he received an Emmy nomination for Outstanding Continuing or Single Performance by a Supporting Actor in Variety or Music, he chose not to appear as himself, instead using a variety of costumes and accents. When Kermit the Frog told Sellers he could relax and be himself, Peter replied:

"But that, you see, my dear Kermit, would be altogether impossible. I could never be myself ... You see, there is no me. I do not exist ... There used to be a me, but I had it surgically removed".

— Peter Sellers, The Muppet Show, February 1978

Sellers starred alongside Lynne Frederick, Lionel Jeffries and Elke Sommer in Richard Quine's The Prisoner of Zenda, released in May 1979, with 3 roles, including King Rudolf IV and King Rudolf V, who ruled over the small fictional country of Ruritania and Syd Frewin, Rudolf V's half-brother. The movie was generally well received, with Janet Maslin of The New York Times observing how Peter divided "his energies between a serious character and a funny one, but that it was his serious performance which was more impressive". However, Philip French, for The Observer, was unimpressed by the film, describing it as "a mess of porridge, Sellers reveals that he can't draw the line between the sincere and the sentimental".

Later in 1979, Peter starred opposite Shirley MacLaine, Melvyn Douglas and Jack Warden, in the black comedy Being There, as Chance, a mindless, emotionless gardener, who was a TV addict. Sellers had said that he wanted to play the role more than anything else, during a BBC interview back in 1971, having successfully persuaded the author of the book, Jerzy Kosinski, to allow him and director Hal Ashby to make the movie, provided he could write the script.

To remain in character, Peter refused most interview requests during filming, having kept his distance from the other actors. Sellers regarded Chance's walk and voice as being the character's most important attributes, and in preparing for the role, he worked with a tape recorder, either alone or with his wife then with Ashby, to perfect the clear enunciation and flat delivery needed to reveal "the childlike mind behind the words".

Peter described his experience of working on the movie as "so humbling, so powerful", with his co-star Shirley MacLaine having found Sellers "a dream" to work with. Peter's performance was universally lauded by critics, having been regarded by critic Danny Smith as the "crowning triumph of Peter Sellers's remarkable career".

Critic Frank Rich wrote of the acting skill required for the role, with a "schismatic personality that Peter had to convey with strenuous vocal and gestural technique ... A lesser actor would have made the character's mental dysfunction flamboyant and drastic ... his intelligence was always deeper, his onscreen confidence greater, his technique much more finely honed": in achieving this, Sellers "makes the film's fantastic premise credible".

Peter won a Best Actor award at the 51st National Board of Review Awards; the London Critics Circle Film Awards Special Achievement Award, the Best Actor award at the 45th New York Film Critics Circle Awards; and the Best Actor – Musical or Comedy award at the 37th Golden Globe Awards. Sellers was also nominated for the Best Actor award at the 52nd Academy Awards and the Best Actor in a Leading Role award at the 34th British Academy Film Awards.

In March 1980 Peter asked his 15-year-old daughter Victoria what she thought about Being There, who later stated that, "I said yes, I thought it was great but then I said, 'You looked like a little fat old man'. ... he went mad. He threw his drink over me and told me to get the next plane home." His younger daughter Sarah told Sellers what she thought about the incident then he sent her a telegram that read "After what happened this morning with Victoria, I shall be happy if I never hear from you again. I won't tell you what I think of you. It must be obvious. Goodbye, Your Father."

Peter's last movie was The Fiendish Plot of Dr. Fu Manchu, a comedic re-imagining of the eponymous adventure novels by Sax Rohmer, in which Sellers played both police inspector Nayland Smith and Fu Manchu, alongside Helen Mirren and David Tomlinson. The production was troubled before filming even started, with two directors—Richard Quine and John Avildsen—fired before the script had been completed.

Peter was dissatisfied with his portrayal of Manchu, his ill-health often causing delays. Arguments between Sellers and director Piers Haggard led to his being fired at Peter's request, Sellers taking over the direction, with his long-time friend David Lodge directing some sequences. Tom Shales of The Washington Post wrote "an indefensibly inept comedy, it's hard to name another good actor who ever made so many bad movies as Sellers, a comedian of great gifts but ferociously faulty judgment. "Manchu" will take its rightful place alongside such colossally ill-advised washouts as Tell Me Where It Hurts, The Bobo and The Prisoner of Zenda".

Peter's final performances were a series of ads for Barclays Bank, filmed in April 1980 in Ireland, having played Monty Casino, a Jewish con-man. Four adverts were scheduled, but only 3 were filmed, as Sellers collapsed in Dublin, again suffering from heart problems. After 2 days in care, he travelled to the Cannes Film Festival, against the advice of his doctors, where Being There was in competition.

Peter fell ill again in Cannes, returning to his home in Gstaad to work on the script for his next project, Romance of the Pink Panther, before agreeing to undergo an angiogram at the Cedars-Sinai Medical Center in Los Angeles, to see if he was able to undergo open-heart surgery. Spike Milligan believed that Sellers's heart condition had lasted 15 years, having "made life difficult for him and had a debilitating effect on his personality." Sellers's fourth marriage to Frederick collapsed shortly afterwards.

Peter had recently started to rebuild his relationship with his son Michael, after the failure of the latter's marriage, who later said that "it marked the beginning of an all-too-brief closeness between us." Sellers told Michael that "he hated so many things he'd done," including leaving his first wife, Anne, and his infatuation with Sophia Loren, having joked that his epitaph should read "Star of stage, screen and alimony."

Peter arrived in London from Geneva on 21st July 1980, having checked into the Dorchester hotel, before visiting Golders Green Crematorium for the first time, to see his parents' ashes. He'd planned to attend a reunion dinner with his Goon Show partners Spike Milligan and Harry Secombe, scheduled for the evening of 22nd July. On the day of the dinner, Sellers took lunch in his hotel suite, having collapsed shortly afterwards from a heart attack. He was taken to the Middlesex Hospital, London, where he died just after midnight on 24th July 1980, aged 54.

Following Peter's death, fellow actor Richard Attenborough said that Sellers "had the genius comparable to Chaplin", while the Boulting brothers regarded Peter as "a man of enormous gifts; and these gifts he gave to the world. For them, he is assured of a place in the history of art as entertainment."

Burt Kwouk, who appeared as Cato in the Pink Panther movies, stated that "Peter was a well-loved actor in Britain ... the day he died, it seemed that the whole country came to a stop. Everywhere you went, the fact that Peter had died seemed like an umbrella over everything". Director Blake Edwards said that "Peter was brilliant. He had an enormous facility for finding really unusual, unique facets of the character he was playing".

Sellers's friend and Goon Show colleague Spike Milligan was too upset to speak to the press at the time of Peter's death, while fellow Goon Harry Secombe said "I'm shattered. Peter was such a tremendous artist. He had so much talent, it just oozed out of him." With black humour, referring to the missed dinner the Goons had planned, he added, "Anything to avoid paying for dinner".

Secombe later said to journalists "Bluebottle is deaded now" then Milligan stated "it's hard to say this, but he died at the right time." The Daily Mail described Sellers as "the greatest comic talent of his generation, as well as a womanising drug-taker, who married 4 times, in a fruitless search for happiness, a flawed genius," who once he latched on to a comic idea, "loved nothing more than to carry it to extremes".

A private funeral service was held at Golders Green Crematorium on 26th July, conducted by Peter's old friend, Canon John Hester. Sellers's final joke was the playing of "In the Mood" by Glenn Miller, a tune he hated. His body was cremated then his ashes were interred at the Crematorium. After her death in 1994, the ashes of his widow Lynne Frederick were co-interred with his. A memorial service was held at St Martin-in-the-Fields on 8th September 1980, what would've been Peter's 55th birthday. His close friend Lord Snowdon read the twenty-third Psalm, Harry Secombe sang "Bread of Heaven" and the eulogy was read by David Niven.

Although Sellers was apparently in the process of excluding Frederick from his will a week before he died, she inherited almost his entire estate, worth an estimated £4.5 million, while his children received just £800 each. Spike Milligan appealed to her on behalf of Peter's 3 children, but she refused to increase the amount. Sellers's only son, Michael, died of a heart attack aged 52 during surgery, on 24th July 2006, 26 years to the day after his father's death.

After his death, Metro-Goldwyn-Mayer tried to continue with Romance of the Pink Panther, having offered the role of Clouseau to Dudley Moore, who turned it down. The studio then returned to Blake Edwards, who was adamant that the character shouldn't be recast, feeling that no one could adequately replace Peter.

In 1982 Edwards released Trail of the Pink Panther, which was composed entirely of deleted scenes from his past 3 Panther films. Frederick sued, claiming the use of the clips was a breach of contract, the court having awarded her $1 million, plus 3.15% of the film's profits and 1.36% of its gross revenue.

"I start with the voice. I find out how the character sounds. It's through the way he speaks that I find out the rest about him. ... After the voice comes the looks of the man. I do a lot of drawings of the character I play. Then I get together with the makeup man and we sort of transfer my drawings onto my face. An involved process. After that I establish how the character walks. Very important, the walk. And then, suddenly, something strange happens. The person takes over. The man you play begins to exist."

— Sellers describing how he prepared for his wide range of roles, in an October 1962 interview for Playboy.

Vincent Canby of The New York Times said of the Pink Panther movies, "I'm not sure why Mr. Sellers and Mr. Lom are such a hilarious team, though it may be because each is a fine comic actor, with a special talent for portraying the sort of all-consuming, epic self-absorption that makes slapstick farce initially acceptable—instead of alarming—and finally so funny."

Film critic Elvis Mitchell said that Peter was one of the few comic geniuses who was able to truly hide behind his characters, giving the audience no sense of what he was really like in rea life. A feature of Sellers' characterisations was that regardless of how clumsy or idiotic they were, he ensured that they always retained their dignity.

On his playing of Clouseau, Peter said: "I set out to play Clouseau with great dignity, because I feel that he thinks he is probably one of the greatest detectives in the world. The original script makes him out to be a complete idiot. I thought a forgivable vanity would humanise him and make him kind of touching."

Ed Sikov, observed that because of this retained dignity, Sellers was "the master of playing men who have no idea how ridiculous they are." Social historian Sam Wasson highlighted the complexity of Peter's performances in the Pink Panther movies, which had the effect of alienating Clouseau from his environment.

Wesson considered that "As 'low' and 'high' comedy rolled into one, it was the performative counterpoint to Edwardian sophisticated naturalism". This combination of "high" and "low", exemplified by Clouseau's attempting to retain dignity after a fall, meant that within the film Clouseau was "the sole representative of humanity".

Movie critic Dilys Powell also saw the inherent dignity in the parts, writing that Sellers had a "balance between character and absurdity". Richard Attenborough also thought that because of his sympathy, Peter could "inject into his characterisations, the frailty and substance of a human being".

Author Aaron Sultanik observed of Sellers's early movies, including I'm All Right Jack, his "deft, technical interpretations pinpoint the mechanical nature of his comic characterization... reduces each of his characters to a series of gross, awkward tics". Academic Cynthia Baron said that Peter's external characterisations led to doubt with reviewers, as to whether Sellers' work was "true" acting.

Critic Tom Milne saw a change over Sellers's career, having thought that his "comic genius as a character actor was ... stifled by his elevation to leading man," with his later films suffering as a result. Sultanik agreed, believing that Peter's "exceptional vocal and physical technique" was under-used during his career in the US.

Academics Maria Pramaggiore and Tom Wallis believed that Sellers fitted the mould of a technical actor, because he displayed a mastery of physical characterisation, such as accent or physical trait. Writer and playwright John Mortimer saw the process for himself when Peter was about to start filming on Mortimer's The Dock Brief but couldn't decide how to play the character of the barrister.

By chance he ordered cockles for lunch, the smell having brought back a memory of the seaside town of Morecambe, which gave him "the idea of a faded North Country accent and the suggestion of a scrappy moustache". So important was the voice as the starting point for character development that Sellers would walk around London with a reel-to-reel tape recorder, recording voices to study at home.

New York magazine stated that the movies starring Peter as Clouseau showcased his "comedic brilliance". Sellers's friend and Goon Show colleague Spike Milligan said that he "had one of the most glittering comic talents of his age", while John and Roy Boulting stated that he was "the greatest comic genius this country has produced since Charles Chaplin". Irv Slifkin said that Peter was the most prominent face in comedies of the sixties, who "changed like a chameleon throughout the era, dazzling audiences".

In a 2005 poll to find "The Comedian's Comedian", Sellers was voted # 14 in the list of the top 20 greatest comedians by fellow comics and comedy insiders. Peter and The Goon Show were a strong influence on Monty Python, and Peter Cook, who described Sellers as "the best comic actor in the world".

The British actor Stephen Mangan stated that Sellers had been a big influence on him, as did the comedians Alan Carr and Rob Brydon. The comic performer Sacha Baron Cohen, famed as Ali G and Borat, referred to Peter as "the most seminal force in shaping my early ideas on comedy". Cohen was considered for the role of Sellers in the biographical film The Life and Death of Peter Sellers.

The 3 members of Spinal Tap—Michael McKean, Christopher Guest and Harry Shearer— also cited Peter as being an influence on them, as did the American talk-show host Conan O'Brien and David Schwimmer, who said : "he could do anything, from Dr Strangelove to Inspector Clouseau. He was just amazing."

Eddie Izzard observed that the Goons "influenced a new generation of comedians, who came to be known as 'alternative,'" including himself, while the media historian Graham McCann stated that "the anarchic spirit of the Goon Show ... would inspire, directly or indirectly and to varying extents, ... The Hitchhiker's Guide to the Galaxy, The Young Ones, Vic Reeves Big Night Out, The League of Gentlemen and Brass Eye."

In 1998, the stage play Being Sellers premiered in Australia, 3 years after the release of the biography by Roger Lewis, The Life and Death of Peter Sellers, the play moving to New York in December 2010. In 2004, the book was turned into an HBO movie of the same title, starring Geoffrey Rush. The Belfast Telegraph observed how the film captured Peter's "life of drugs, drink, fast cars and lots and lots of beautiful women".

Although the movie was widely praised by critics, both Lord Snowdon and Britt Ekland were highly critical of the film and it's depiction of Sellers. Ekland believed that the movie left audiences with the wrong idea about her former husband, saying "the film leaves you with the impression that Peter Sellers was essentially a likeable man, when in reality he was a monster. He may have been a brilliant actor, but as a human being he had no saving graces at all".

Snowdon disagreed with both Britt's verdict, and with the movie, having stated that Sellers "had a light touch, a sense of humour, I can't bear to see him portrayed as somebody who was apparently without either ... The man on the screen is charmless, humourless and boring—the one thing you could never say about Peter."

Filmography, with selected other works, based on award nominations

Film Year Role Award

The Running Jumping & Standing Still Film 1959 Nominated – Academy Award for Short Subject (Live Action)

I'm All Right Jack 1959 Fred Kite Won – British Academy Film Award for Best British Actor

Waltz of the Toreadors 1962 General Leo Fitzjohn Won – San Sebastián International Film Festival for Best Actor

Lolita 1962 Clare Quilty Nominated – Golden Globe Award for Best Supporting Actor

Only Two Can Play 1962 John Lewis Nominated – British Academy Film Award for Best British Actor

The Pink Panther 1963 Inspector Jacques Clouseau Nominated – Golden Globe Award for Best Actor – Musical or Comedy

Nominated – British Academy Film Award for Best British Actor

Dr. Strangelove or: How I Learned to Stop Worrying and Love the Bomb 1964 Group Captain Lionel Mandrake/President Merkin Muffley/Dr. Strangelove Nominated – Academy Award for Best Actor

Nominated – British Academy Film Award for Best British Actor

The Optimists of Nine Elms 1973 Sam Won – Tehran Film Festival Award for Best Actor

The Return of the Pink Panther 1975 Inspector Jacques Clouseau Won – The Evening News British Film Award for Best Actor

Nominated – Golden Globe Award for Best Actor – Musical or Comedy

The Pink Panther Strikes Again 1976 Inspector Jacques Clouseau Nominated – Golden Globe Award for Best Actor – Musical or Comedy

Being There 1979 Chance Won – National Board of Review Award for Best Actor

Won – New York Film Critics Circle Award for Best Actor

Won – Golden Globe Award for Best Actor – Musical or Comedy

Won – London Film Critics Circle Award for Best Actor

Nominated – British Academy Film Award for Best Actor in a Leading Role

Nominated – Academy Award for Best Actor

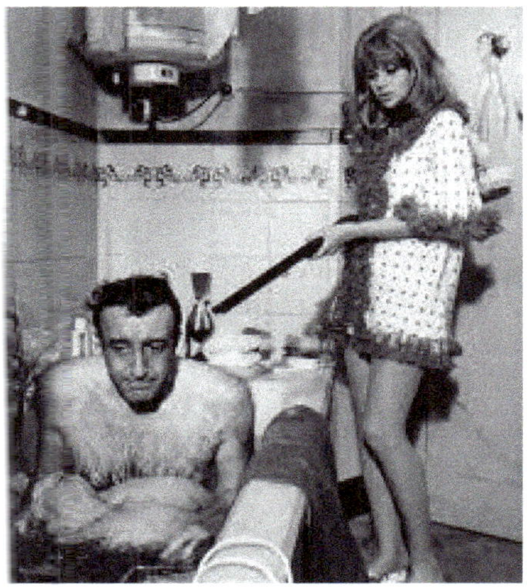

ADFORD
RADFORD

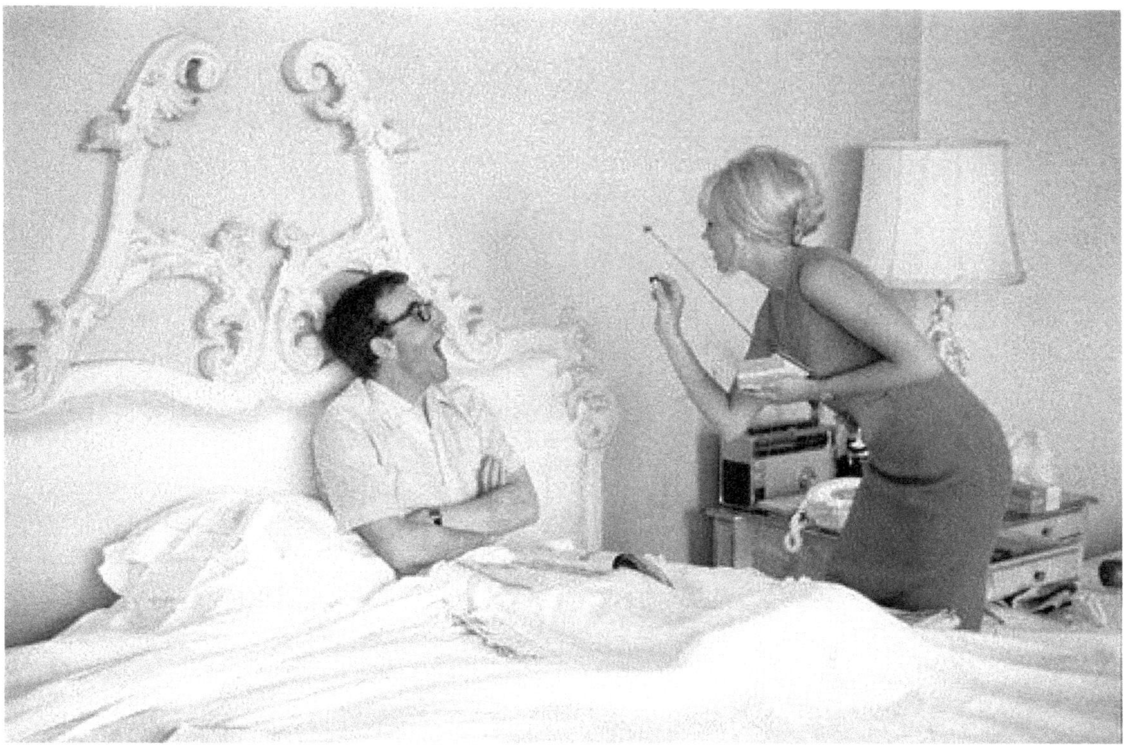

RADFORD
RADFORD

FOTOPICS

VARIETY
'MY SON, THE TV EXECUTIVE'

Britt Ekland, born Britt-Marie Eklund on 6th October 1942, Stockholm, Sweden is an actress and singer. Britt appeared in many films during her heyday of the 1960s and 1970s, including critically acclaimed roles in William Friedkin's The Night They Raided Minsky's (1968), then the British crime movie Get Carter (1971), which established her as a big screen sex symbol.

Ekland also starred in the British cult horror film The Wicker Man (1973), before appearing as a Bond girl in The Man with the Golden Gun (1974). Britt's high-profile social life and her 1964 marriage to actor Peter Sellers, attracted intense media attention, leading to her being one of the world's most photographed celebrities during the 1970s.

Ekland was the daughter of Maj Britt, a secretary, and Sven Axel Eklund, who ran an upscale clothing store in Stockholm, having also captained the Swedish national curling team. Ekland's mother died of Alzheimer's disease during the 1980s, which deeply affected her. Britt grew up with three younger brothers, having said that she was overweight for much of her childhood:

"I was very heavy. God, I was brutal-looking. I always tried to be funny to make up for the fact that I was fat and ugly." As a teenager, Ekland left school to travel with a theatre company, having been spotted by a talent agent in a coffee shop while in Italy, who sent her to London to audition for films.

Britt began her career with bit parts and uncredited walk-on roles, including her first onscreen role in G.I. Blues (1960), which was followed with a small supporting part in The Happy Thieves (1960). Ekland had short parts in the Swedish movies Kort är sommaren (1962) and Det är hos mig han har varit (1963), before being given her first major supporting role in the George Marshall Western, Advance to the Rear (1964).

In 1964, Britt appeared in the Christmas TV film, A Carol for Another Christmas, when she met her future husband, Peter Sellers, her co-star. Ekland followed this with After the Fox (1966) then The Bobo (1967), both also starring Sellers. Britt then had a lead role as an Amish girl turned New York City burlesque dancer, in William Friedkin's musical The Night They Raided Minsky's (1968), for which she received critical acclaim. Her next movie was Stiletto (1969), a crime drama, based on a novel by Harold Robbins, co-starring Alex Cord, before she starred in a string of Italian films, Machine Gun McCain (1969), The Conspirators (1969), and as Antigone in The Cannibals (1970).

In 1971, Ekland was cast in the leading rôle of gun moll in the iconic crime movie Get Carter, opposite Michael Caine, firmly establishing her as a blonde bombshell. In the 1970s Britt also starred in several horror films, including What the Peeper Saw (1972) as a disturbed bride, followed by the Agatha Christie adaptation Endless Night (1972), playing the friend and companion of an American heiress then as a hallucinatory figure in the anthology movie Asylum (1972), opposite Charlotte Rampling. Ekland's most iconic role came in the 1973 cult horror film The Wicker Man, in which she played a Pagan villager and seductress, her voice being dubbed to disguise her Swedish-accented English.

Britt's other movies included the The Ultimate Thrill (1974), which followed the British drama Baxter! (1973) and the TV film The Six Million Dollar Man: Wine, Women and War (1973) opposite Lee Majors. Ekland's next prominent role was as the lead Bond girl, Mary Goodnight, in the James Bond movie, The Man with the Golden Gun (1974), which despite receiving mixed reviews strengthened her status as a sex symbol.

In 1976 Britt provided the French spoken part, at the end of then boyfriend Rod Stewart's hit single "Tonight's the Night (Gonna Be Alright)". Ekland also portrayed biographical characters, including one based on real-life actress Anny Ondra, boxer Max Schmeling's wife, in the TV movie, Ring of Passion (1978). Britt was also featured in the horror film, The Monster Club (1980) and Satan's Mistress (1982). Ekland then had supporting roles in independent movies, having appeared in the comedy Fraternity Vacation (1985), followed by the slasher film Moon in Scorpio (1988) then as prostitute Mariella Novotny, in the feature film Scandal (1989), about the Profumo Affair.

Britt has guest-starred in several TV series, including the popular Superboy, playing an alien disguised as Lara, Superboy's biological mother, during the show's second season in 1990. Ekland published a beauty and fitness book, Sensual Beauty: How to Achieve It (1984), followed by a fitness video in 1992. She hosted the 1971 episode of the BBC TV series, I Love the '70s (1999), in homage to her role as "Anna" in the film Get Carter.

Britt's later career has largely comprised stage and TV work, her last movie role having been in The Children (1990). She appeared on stage in Cinderella at the Regent Theatre, Stoke-on-Trent in December 1999 and January 2000. Ekland also appeared in Grumpy Old Women Live, and took part in the Swedish reality show Stjärnorna på slottet (The stars at the castle) in December 2007 along with Peter Stormare, Arja Saijonmaa, Jan Malmsjö and Magnus Härenstam, then later that month she starred again in Cinderella, at the Wyvern Theatre, Swindon.

Britt appeared as a guest on the British daytime TV show Loose Women, in January 2008 then from December 2008 to January 2009 starred in Cinderella, at the Shaw Theatre in London. A rare singing performance was of the song My Prince, originally recorded by Lara Pulver on the album Act One – Songs from the Musicals of Alexander S. Bermange.

In 2009–10, Ekland played the Fairy Godmother in Cinderella at Princess Theatre, Torquay followed in December 2010 by the 'Fairy Pea Pod,' in Jack and the Beanstalk, at the Kings Theatre, Southsea. Britt then starred in further Pantomimes at the Theatre Royal, Windsor, in 2011 and 2012.

In 2010 Ekland took part in the ITV reality show I'm a Celebrity...Get Me Out of Here! when she was fourth to be voted off. During the program she developed a close relationship with Stacey Solomon and Nigel Havers, while making an enemy of Gillian McKeith. Ekland was one of the housewives of Svenska Hollywoodfruar (Swedish Hollywoodwives) on TV3, during the 2013 season. Britt was in Let's Dance 2018, broadcast on TV4, having been the first of the 11 celebrities to be eliminated on 30 March.

Ekland became famous due to her whirlwind romance and marriage to English actor and comedian, Peter Sellers in 1964, who proposed after seeing her photograph in the paper then meeting her in London. In January 1965 they had a daughter, Victoria, but Peter suffered a series of heart attacks shortly after their marriage. Britt was stepmother to Sellers' children Sarah and Michael, who died of a heart attack at the same age as his father. The couple made three films together — A Carol for Another Christmas (1964), After the Fox (1966) and The Bobo (1967), before divorcing in 1968.

In June 1973, Ekland had a son, Nic Adler, with record producer Lou Adler. Britt also had a much publicised romance with rock star Rod Stewart, following their introduction by Joan Collins in 1975, having lived together for more than two years, with Ekland giving up her career to focus on the relationship.

From 1979–1981, Britt dated then became engaged to Girl frontman and future L.A. Guns singer Phil Lewis. In 1984 she married Stray Cats drummer Slim Jim Phantom, who was 19 years younger than her, aged 23. They had a son, Thomas Jefferson in 1988, before divorcing in 1992.

In the 1970s, Ekland was one of the most photographed and talked-about celebrities in the world. In 1980, her best-selling autobiography, True Britt, was published. While Rod Stewart's partner, Ekland inspired his hit song Tonight's the Night (Gonna Be Alright), 1977's #1 song, featuring a French spoken part by Britt. In 2004, Ekland was portrayed by Charlize Theron in The Life and Death of Peter Sellers, having accompanied Theron to the Cannes Film Festival where she became highly emotional when she saw the film.

Filmography

Film

Year Title Role Notes

1960 G.I. Blues Britta uncredited

1962 The Happy Thieves Mrs. Pickett

Kort är sommaren Edvarda's Friend

1963 Il comandante Iris

Det är hos mig han har varit Li's Workmate

The Devil uncredited

The Prize nudist

1964 Advance to the Rear Greta

A Carol for Another Christmas mother

Sonaron cuatro balazos

1965 Do Not Disturb Party girl uncredited

1966 After the Fox Gina Romantica

1967 The Double Man Gina

Too Many Thieves Claudia

The Bobo Olimpia Segura

1968 The Night They Raided Minsky's Rachel Schpitendavel

1969 Stiletto Illeana

Machine Gun McCain Irene Tucker

The Conspirators Princess Spada

1970 The Year of the Cannibals Antigone

Tintomara Adolphine

1971 Percy Dorothy Chiltern-Barlow

Get Carter Anna

The Stronger woman 1 TV film

1972 A Time for Loving Josette Papillion

Night Hair Child Elise

Endless Night Greta

Asylum Lucy

1973 Baxter! Chris Bentley

The Wicker Man Willow

The Six Million Dollar Man: Wine, Women and War Katrina Volana TV film

1974 The Ultimate Thrill Michelle Parlay

The Man with the Golden Gun Mary Goodnight

1975 Royal Flash Dutchess Irma

1976 High Velocity Mrs. Andersen

1977 Casanova & Co. Countess Trivulzi

1978 Slavers Anna von Erken

The Great Wallendas Jenny Wallenda TV film

1979 King Solomon's Treasure Queen Nyleptha

1980 The Monster Club Busotsky's Mother

The Hostage Tower Leah

1981 Jacqueline Susann's Valley of the Dolls Françoise Mini-series

1982 Satan's Mistress Ann-Marie

1983 Dr. Yes: Hyannis Affair Susannah

Dead Wrong Penny Lancaster

Erotic Images Julie Todd

1984 Love Scenes Annie

1985 Fraternity Vacation Eyvette

Marbella, un golpe de cinco estrellas Deborah

1986 Az aranyifjú Mrs. Pidlington TV film

1987 Moon in Scorpio Linda

1989 Scandal Mariella Novotny

Cold Heat Jackie Mallon

Beverly Hills Vamp Madame Cassandra

Television

Year Title Role Notes

1965 Armchair Theatre Karen Episode: "A Cold Peace"

1966 The Trials of O'Brien Claudia Episodes: "The Greatest Game, Part 1; 2"

1970 The Dean Martin Show herself Episode: "6.3"

1971 Aquarius Mrs. X Strindberg's Stronger/LS.Lowry/Liverpool's Kop

1972-77 McCloud Tatiana Krasnavian / Vicki Erickson Episodes: "The Barefoot Stewardess Caper," "The Moscow Connection"

1978 Battlestar Galactica Tenna Episodes: "Gun on Ice Planet Zero: Part 1; 2"

1979 Return of the Saint Laura Episode: "The Murder Cartel"

Skeppsredaren Patricia

1980-82 The Love Boat Alice Robbins / Karen EllisonEpisodes: "Vicki's First Love/The High Cost of Loving/Accident Prone", "Doc Take the Fifth/Safety Last/A Business Affair"

1982 Matt Houston Vera Martin Episode: "Deadly Fashion"

1980-83 Fantasy Island Linda / Clarissa Bevis / Berniece Williams / Aphrodite Four episodes

1984 The Fall Guy herself Episode: "Always Say Always"

1985 Simon & Simon Samantha BlakeEpisode: "Love and/or Marriage"

1990 Superboy Lara Lor-Van Episodes: "Escape to Earth," "Abandon Earth"

Grand Viveca Episode: "Blow Off"

1992 Bara med Britt herself / host

1994 Absolutely Fabulous herself Episode: "New Best Friend"

1997 Brass Eye herself Episode: "Animals"

2002 Lexx Dulcibella Sternflanks Episode: "Prime Ridge"

2010 I'm a Celebrity...Get Me Out of Here! herself / contestant 20 episodes

2013 Astrid in Wonderland herself Episode #5.8

2013–2015 Svenska Hollywoodfruar herself

2018 Let's Dance herself / contestant 2 episodes

Discography

"Do it to Me once more (with feeling)" / "Private Party" (1979) No. 15 SWE

Britt Ekland swept into the lobby of the hotel, her long platinum blonde hair swinging as she walked. She was wearing a black chiffon top and black-and-gold skinny jeans, with her Chihuahua, Tequila, perched in her handbag. Britt was wearing the darkest of glasses, the reason for which became clear when she removed them, as the white of her left eye was bright blood red, a startling contrast to her cornflower blue pupils. Ekland said she'd just poked her eye out with a pen while she was holding on to 2 phones. It looked shocking and painful but she shrugged it off, as compared to what she'd been through, it was nothing.

Britt had most famously survived a jealousy fuelled, destructive marriage to Peter Sellers, having married after they'd known each other for only 10 days. She was with Rod Stewart for 8 years but he cheated on her so she left him. She had her 3rd child aged 46, with her 2nd husband, Stray Cat rocker Slim Jim Phantom, with whom she broke up in 1992.

Ekland became a much sought after sex symbol following her starring role as a Bond Girl in The Man with the Golden Gun (1973), but aged 70 she mainly lived in Los Angeles, a town where almost everyone over 27 was apparently invisible. The past few years had been hard going, with many pantomimes in Britain and a stint on I'm a Celebrity Get Me Out of Here, from which most celebrities emerged from the experience to talk philosophically about its life changing learning curve.

What did she get from it? "Nothing except a urinary tract infection," she laughed, it having been a consequence of spending the night on a rain-soaked bed. Sitting in a smart cabana by the pool, Britt began talking about a reality TV show she'd just finished filming – Swedish Hollywood Wives. "Very hard work, when you're an actress you have a script, a director, someone doing your make-up. Here you do everything yourself. Make-up, costume, script – you decide what to do. You can never relax because the camera is always there. You've got a microphone glued to your body in between your breasts."

Her breasts! Rather a lot of those were seen in the newly restored director's cut of the The Wicker Man (1973). Dubbed "the Citizen Kane of horror movies", it was about an uptight policeman, Edward Woodward, who was manipulated by a pagan community on a Hebridean island. Ekland's character engaged in a lot of pagan-style naked dancing: "Yes, those were my breasts," Britt clarified.

They were gigantic! "Yes they were very, very impressive. I think that's why I got the Bond film. I can't verify this because Cubby is now dead but it must have been. I was pregnant with my son. My son who is now going to have a baby." The baby, Cassius, was born not long after. He had 3 grandmothers: Ekland, its mother's mother, and Paige Hannah, wife of record producer Lou Adler, with whom Britt had her son.

"All three of us went to a grandmother and wine class to learn how to become grandmothers. It was a two-hour class. Everything you know already, except today you don't hold a baby like this" – she did a rocking motion – "you hold it like this, like a football." She demonstrated an American footballer. "Apparently that will stop them crying immediately. I think it would stop me too." It can't have been easy growing old in public, a photograph every time you went out without make-up or your face looked saggy. Ekland stayed fit with Pilates and by running backwards, which she swore burned 20% more calories than running forwards.

She'd never been entirely comfortable with the way she looked, and for The Wicker Man's copious bum shots a body double was used. "I've never liked my bottom, so it was another bottom that was out there freezing on the moors. It was really freezing doing that naked dancing." It was so cold that the cast had to suck on ice cubes, to stop their breath from showing.

"I went down to London on my day off, because my skirts weren't fitting me properly, so I thought I should have a pregnancy test. It turned out I was 4 months pregnant when I was swanning about in The Wicker Man and when I came back from the doctor they had hired a stunt bottom. I had no idea they would do that, I just stipulated I would not do naked from behind.

Naked, in any case, it's not my favourite thing but you've got to give a little bit," she said with a sly grin. It was hard not to conjure up the image of her breasts knocking against the wall, where Edward Woodward was in his pyjamas in the other room. "He was totally uninterested," she said.

He did look hot and bothered. "I think that was acting. Christopher Lee and he were both very closed, dour people. I can get along with anyone, with a snail, but these people I could not reach. I hated being on the movie, because I was pregnant and it was hard and because Robin Hardy didn't like me. He wanted Ingrid Pitt to have my role, because she was having an affair with both the producer of the film and the head of the distribution company.

I remember when we were out there on the moors in our long, flowing gowns and she was running like we all had to, but she was running in this brand new Cartier watch. She wouldn't take it off. I would have to say, 'Ingrid, pull down your sleeve so they can't see your watch.' I certainly didn't want to re-shoot on the moors. It was a tough shoot and I didn't do anything to promote it, because I was heavily pregnant then the film disappeared, but then it came back and I don't feel it ever went away."

Britt was 30 when she played the role of Willow but she looked much younger than that with her giant blue eyes, cherubic face and long blonde hair. "I did look younger and I always felt that was a problem. When we're young we want to look old and sophisticated. At 16 I started smoking to seem older but that didn't help."

When Ekland was 20 she met Peter Sellers then married him within a fortnight. She still had no idea why. "I never wanted to marry. I thought that marriage was a lousy institution and women had a really tough deal." Then why do it? "I was very young and he swept me off my feet. He gave me a puppy for God's sake. What was he thinking? And what was I thinking? You can't bring up a dog before you've brought up yourself.

It was a terrible thing to do. It's like giving someone a Teddy Bear that also happens to be alive and he gave me a dog when I was staying at the Dorchester but the thing that worries me most now is I can't remember what happened to that puppy. It was a little dachshund. I can't just have left it at the Dorchester when I moved out but I don't know where it is. I didn't know anyone in England, not a single sausage, because I'd just come from Sweden. My big worry today is what happened to that little dachshund." Perhaps she didn't have time to think about the puppy, because of the speed at which their relationship hurtled along. Married in February, pregnant by April, with her daughter Victoria.

"I told all my children: don't do what I did. Meet someone, travel with them, go on holiday, have fun, party. Don't fall in love and have a baby. So they didn't. My son is 40 having his first baby. He took the advice very seriously and Victoria is not going to have any children now.

She's too old, but she didn't want any. My youngest is 25 and much too young to think about it."

Where she was naive, Sellers was compulsive and jealous beyond all reason. He would be watching a movie with Brigitte Bardot in it, doing a love scene then suddenly he would imagine it was Britt in bed with another man. Britt, Brigitte, blonde, almost the same. Did she think he was madly in love or just mad?

"I think today we would say he was bipolar, although that word is bandied about so often. He had mental problems and he should have been in therapy. If I'd met him today I would know so much more, but I didn't. I had no experience of that sort of life but I learnt very quickly." Ekland had been discovered by a talent scout for 20th Century Fox then signed to a 7-picture deal.

"I was working in London with Richard Attenborough and he [Sellers] was working in LA on a movie. It was Easter 1964, March, and he said, 'Why don't you take one day off and come over.' I asked and they said no and he said, 'I will fix everything, just take your passport.' He had a car pick me up at the studio telling me I'd be back on Monday, so I left with my handbag and I never went back. Fox sued me and put me on suspension for 2 years, so I couldn't work and then I lost my contract. He made sure I stayed with him. He hadn't fixed anything for me; he just made sure I didn't go back.

You see things on the news all the time about people being abducted. It felt like that." Sellers was 17 years her senior and she'd lived a very sheltered existence. Really, though? How could she have been that naive? "I know, I know... Of course I shouldn't have married. I should have waited and continued my career."

Britt still had no explanation for her part in the madness, but she proffered, "I didn't marry Lou Adler or Rod Stewart. I've only been married to Peter Sellers and Slim Jim Phantom. We are good friends. I really love him. That's the thing with love. You might be hurt but ultimately if they are good people a friendship stays. Jim was never unfaithful, Lou was, and at the time I thought that was unforgivable. Now I think there are worse things.

"Rod was unfaithful and he didn't get another chance. I told him because I was very much in love with him that if he was unfaithful that would be the end of our relationship and it was. He couldn't help himself, it was like a kid in a candy store." Warren Beatty was said to have been her boyfriend at one point.

"No, it was just an intense shag session and that was it." Was he good in bed? "At the time I thought he was. I was young and I thought it was very exciting, someone you had a crush on, a movie star who turned out to be real. It was a great fantasy but it wasn't real life. I'm not sure if I really discovered my sexual self till my thirties but I'm not really sure, as even that was such a long time ago. I don't have any lovers now. I don't know if I could put up with lovers.

In the old days bachelors were men who had the best of everything. They had girlfriends. They ate and drank and skied and went to the south of France and drove beautiful cars. They were set in their ways, they weren't gay, they just didn't want to get married and that's where I am today. I am like an old-fashioned bachelor." When she was that girl in The Wicker Man, dancing, so carefree and without self-consciousness, how did she envisage her future?

"I never thought I'd live beyond 40, because I thought 40 was very old. I never expected my life to go this far. When I was young I thought I would be engaged, have the ring, get married, and then have a wedding ring, everything proper. That's not how it happened." Perhaps that was because she fell for crazy actors and rock stars?

"I do love music and my life would be worthless unless I had music in it. Lou was a record producer, Rod a singer, and Jim the drummer. It was just a coincidence. I didn't go for them on purpose. All I knew is that I didn't want to get involved with another actor again. They are much too vain and self-absorbed and I never did get involved with another one.

I wouldn't want a man who is fighting in the morning for the mirror. All the men in my life were very much men. Not necessarily macho, but secure in their place as a man and I've always been the fluffy blonde who didn't want to be fluffy. I look at pictures on the internet. I find these incredible pictures of me that I've never seen. Some I have a vague memory of. I never thought I looked any good at the time."

In 1996, she auctioned most of her memorabilia: "I separated from Jim and my house in London was so full, I couldn't move for art nouveau. I sold everything then I became minimalistic," she said. Ekland sold Gucci handbags given to her by Sellers, crocodile shoes from Dior, silver Art Nouveau picture frames, and a snakeskin full-length coat, made especially for her by Ossie Clark.

"He lived around the corner from me in London and one day asked if he could borrow the coat, because he wanted to use it in a show, so it never made it to the auction. I was out one night when Ossie brought the coat back and that was the night he was killed. Very, very sad. So that coat went in the sale as well." Britt's mother suffered from Alzheimer's, so she became an ambassador for the Alzheimer's Society, saying the one thing that she feared in life was getting an illness that she "can't control".

"My mum got it in her fifties and was 78 when she died. That makes no sense. The rest of her was incredibly healthy. If that happened to me I would will myself dead. I would say I want to die. I want to die, and He upstairs would have to listen to me, because my mum's illness was too horrible for words. There are things you can do – like take them out all winter, so they catch pneumonia then do nothing – but we didn't do that. It would be horrifying if my kids kept me alive like we kept my mum alive."

Her daughter, Victoria Sellers, was linked with the Hollywood madame Heidi Fleiss, with whom she made a video, Sex Tips with Heidi Fleiss and Victoria Sellers. She also had a couple of short stints in prison, one for receiving stolen goods, the second for being in possession of amphetamines but following a cocktail-making course paid for by her mother, she was working as a bartender.

"She is in a nice restaurant Monday to Friday. She wears a white shirt, black tie, black waistcoat and black pants. None of that," she gestured, fluttering her fingers, to indicate low-cut, skimpy attire. Her life is very together. She also designs jewellery but she couldn't support herself doing just that.

She works back to back and does outside catering weekends and sometimes she works as my assistant in the show [Swedish Hollywood Wives]. She is a loving and very special person. She has always helped me. If she has a day off, I say get this and this. I pay her because I know what it's like not being paid."

What else did Ekland have coming up? "I'm going to star in the biggest production in my life. The role of grandmother. No panto for me this year." Instead she'd be at home with her family, decorating the tree. "I want to be there holding the baby, loving and old-fashioned."

To understand the meaning of Swedish starlet Britt Ekland, if one pictured the entertainment world as Mount Everest, with all its male sex symbols as slalom poles, Britt held the Olympic record for the Giant Slalom of Love. Since her early marriage to Peter Sellers, she'd swirled through a dizzying series of affairs with some of the most celebrated ladykillers around—

Warren Beatty, Ryan O'Neal, movie-record tycoon Lou Adler. Then came her tumultuous 3 years as the blonde on Rod Stewart's arm, which was the finish line.

Ekland came to realize that she was on a strictly downhill course, as at 37 she was getting pretty old to be a starlet. Over the previous couple of years she'd tried to make her name in showbiz. Despite 25 movie credits, with the most distinguished probably being The Night They Raided Minsky's, the best she'd been offered lately had been CBS' upcoming disaster epic, The Hostage Tower.

In TV series her rudder seemed stuck on Fantasy Island and Love Boat. In December 1978 she'd tried the London stage in a play called Mate! which lasted only 3 weeks on the West End. She'd released her first record in Europe, a disco single, Do It to Me, which might never have gone gold but was already blue, being a picture-disc with her nude image pressed into both sides.

However, anyone who thought Britt had played her last trump card hadn't been paying attention to the showbiz marketplace for memoirs. Enter British literary agent and ghostwriter Don Short. Britt, who was far from the vacuous victim that she'd sometimes been depicted, just happened to have been keeping a diary since she was 14.

So with that to help bring back her memories, she sat down with Short from 10 a.m. to 11 p.m. for two months. He said "Britt would get weepy and upset then disappear to compose herself. That was usually when she was talking about Sellers." Ekland added "It was like being in therapy."

The book itself, titled True Britt, was being published that summer in London, with serialized excerpts of the juiciest parts of the 40 audio cassettes and 1,000-page transcript having created a sensation in Europe. Agent Short estimated world serialization rights at $500,000, the auction for U.S. publishers beginning, with no bid under $100,000 being accepted.

Nearly all the men who'd found themselves publicly short-sheeted had remained silent, in addition to the Hollywood names, having included Britain's Lord Lichfield, a cousin of the Queen. The exception was Peter Sellers, who'd asked London courts to block publication of Britt's marital indiscretions but then withdrew, saying "She's a professional girlfriend and an amateur actress." Did Ekland have any second thoughts? "I have nothing to hide anymore," she said. Short stated "She was very concerned about hurting people's feelings. She also hasn't avoided embarrassing people who need to be embarrassed."

Among those apparently taking it like a brick were Britt's own parents back in Stockholm. As she'd recounted in her autobiography, Ekland grew up the only daughter in a genteel family of four. Her mother, Maj Britt, was once a secretary. Her father, Sven Axel Eklund, ran the family's elegant clothing store, later becoming captain of the Swedish national curling team then the president of the International Curling Association.

Britt recalled growing up "very heavy. God, I was brutal-looking. I always tried to be funny to make up for the fact that I was fat and ugly." However, by the time she left private school to tour with a theatre company, she was a Nordic beauty. A 20th Century-Fox talent scout spotted her in Italy then sent her to London to audition for a film.

There she met Sellers, who was 38, she was 21, the couple being married within 11 days. Even during the first honeymoon months, Ekland stated, the moody Sellers set spies to watch her, while he was away on movie location. Later, she alleged, during a quarrel he demanded that she abort their child but she refused. One night Britt was late returning from Elstree Studios then the next morning found that Sellers had smashed her gold Cartier watch, having tried to flush it down the toilet. In their 1967 film collaboration, The Bobo, Ekland was cast as a scheming gold digger.

Ekland debunked the widely reported romantic legend that Peter's near-fatal 1964 heart attack occurred while they were making love, saying, "We were drinking champagne in bed, watching TV, and we spilled the champagne. I was changing the bed then as he was bending over, he suddenly went, 'Aaah.' I got him an aspirin and a glass of cognac. The next day in hospital he had seven consecutive attacks."

"Men have basically never been monsters to me except Sellers," Britt went on. She referred to him only by his last name, not having seen or spoken to him in 5 or 6 years. "The only reason I dislike Sellers is for what he's not done for his daughter," said Ekland of Victoria, then aged 15, a student at a Palm Springs private school. "He has sporadically paid child support, but for the last 9 months, nothing. I'll bring her up, but she adores her father, and she needs him desperately."

Britt and Peter were divorced in 1968, with one of the next men in her life having been Warren Beatty. "I fell madly in love with him, which was totally futile, since he was going out with someone else [Julie Christie]. It was such a short affair anyway, just 6 weeks, but then I was in love with him for months and months. He was so handsome, intelligent, witty, kind and flirtatious. He was an incredible lover but I haven't slept with him since 1970, so he may have fallen off since then."

It was different with Ryan O'Neal, whom she and Sellers had double-dated with, back when Ryan was married to Leigh Taylor-Young. "We slept together only 3 or 4 times and he never came to my home, I always went to his hotel. At the time he was in love with Bianca Jagger and they were having a torrid romance, while Mick was abroad." Ekland just sighed of Ryan. "He was very nice."

She spoke less warmly of her breakup from Rod Stewart. "I was really badly hurt when I broke up with Rod," said Britt of the man who dumped her for model Liz Treadwell, before marrying Alana Hamilton, George Hamilton's ex. "I put all my apples in one basket, and I was left out .. He's mean, he knows he's mean. Everybody knows he's mean, it's no secret."

There was a time, though, when her breathily prurient lyrics, dubbed on his Tonight's the Night hit, applied to all their evenings. Ekland revealed other intimacies, including details about groupies, coke-snorting and that Rod wore her cotton panties during performances, because they wouldn't show a seam in his sexy, skintight pants.

She regretted the $12.5 million palimony suit she filed against Stewart. "People are guessing that I'm getting royalties, houses, money, and none of it is true. I can assure you the settlement's not half a million dollars. We signed an agreement never to discuss it." She'd last seen Rod in December, when he and Alana had breezed into a party thrown for her at Paris' Lido 78 disco then sat at the honoree's table. "He didn't even say hello. No one could believe it. I think it was because of her. I've heard he's really hen-pecked and scared."

One of her ex-men who drew Britt's unqualified admiration was Lou Adler, producer ' of groups including the Mamas and the Papas and such movies as Monterey Pop and Up in Smoke. He was the father of her son, Nicholai, 6, and though their four-year relationship ended in 1975, Ekland called him "my best friend in the world. I can tell him anything. He's beautiful, wonderful and loving, and really helps me and cares about his son and Victoria. He's a real human father, not a movie star father." The boy's time was split between his parents, with Nicholai being in Vancouver, where Lou was back on location. Adler, owned the 4-bedroom Bel Air home where Britt lived with her two children and a Norwegian elkhound Zasu.

"We live together as one, somewhat happy family," said Ekland, though she said that Victoria had had "problems from time to time. This is not the place to bring up children. They'll think the whole world lives in Bel Air houses with movie star mothers. You should grow up in a proper household—breakfast, dinner, mother and dad, outings and picnics and movies and zoos." Britt, who had always retained her Swedish citizenship, was still close to her divorced parents, frequently visiting each other.

Despite her domestic side, Ekland hadn't exactly curbed her roaming ways. After Stewart, she'd found brief consolation with Bubba Hettig, a 22-year-old circus aerialist, who she'd met while shooting NBC's The Great Wallendas. Lately she'd become a regular at L.A.'s New Wave rock concerts, having been linked with younger-than-Rod rockers, including John Waite of the Babies. Her one-week fling with Foghat drummer Roger Earl having been two years earlier. "It's a coincidence that some of the people I know have been young, I don't feel there's anything wrong about it."

Two months earlier she'd discovered rollerskating, since having wheeled through Flippers, L.A.'s slickest skate palace, four nights a week. She attended Gilda's Century City exercise class daily, also working out at a Nautilus gym. "I like being in tune," said Britt, who'd given up her once heavy champagne habit and hadn't smoked in 8 months or eaten red meat since 1975. "My body has to last me another couple of years, because I have no other source of income," she said, before hastily clarifying "I never lived with anyone for money. I've fulfilled most of my fantasies, now only my dreams remain."

Peter Sellers was a nightmare to live with, she was desperately in love with Rod Stewart and she had a tattoo in an intimate place. Britt Ekland, as famous for her love life as her films, was disarmingly open. Ask her a personal question then she'd fill in the details as fast as many women her age filled in wrinkles. At 67 she was happy to discuss those too, having had cosmetic surgery, which she said was 'fantastic'.

The former actress, model and legendary Swedish beauty, was about to open her new one-woman show in Wales, during which she promised to be completely candid, taking as many questions as she could. She'd discuss her childhood in Sweden, her doomed marriage to Peter Sellers, relationships with Lou Adler and Rod Stewart, and her second marriage to Slim Jim Phantom of the Stray Cats. When all that was over she'd come up to date, talking about her mother's death from Alzheimer's, before moving on to questions from the audience.

In a world where most celebrities were controlled by stylists and image consultants, Britt's frankness could surely only make her more attractive. Ekland said that as an actress of her age it was very difficult to get good roles. “The last really good part I had was in Grumpy Old Women 2 years ago, so I thought I might as well do something I've produced.”

She was preparing for a month-long, 10 venue tour, after commissioning a writer, having called up lifelong friend Victor Spinetti to direct An Audience With Britt Ekland, “Acting is an ageist, sexist profession and always has been. What can you do? You look at Christopher Lee and Sean Connery both of whom are still working and Christopher must be at least 80. For films and television, as a woman, by the time you're 35 to 40 you're finished.”

Britt didn't say this with any bitterness, just pointing out that she understood the situation. “When I was young I didn't think about it. You live in the moment. I was unaware of the future, I worked, I married and I had children.” Which made it sound a lot less glamorous than it surely was.

Ekland had been in a couple of films by the time she was signed by 20th Century Fox then taken to London aged 21. Stuck in a tiny room in the Dorchester Hotel, she was shocked to get a call from Peter Seller's valet. The filmstar comedian was staying in the same hotel, having seen her photo in that evening's paper, so wanted to meet for a drink.

Britt'd slept with other men but this was a relationship she wasn't ready for. Two weeks after Sellers summoned her to his suite, the couple married. “I was 21 when I married Peter Sellers but I had a mental age of 16. I had never lived with a man, I came straight from my parents. had slept with men but to live and sleep with a man are two completely different things.

It was very, very scary. He was a very difficult man. I think now, with knowledge I've acquired since, that he had manic depression. A lot of comedians do. He was a funny man but it was not funny to live with. When you are young you learn to accept things. It's a terrible analogy but that's how children cope with abuse.”

Ekland's parents, rather than cautioning their beautiful daughter not to rush into marriage with an older man, encouraged it. “Fame is the most seductive thing isn't it ? Your daughter is going to marry this movie star. Wow! He's 18 years older, divorced with two children but he's a name.” She said her father was completely star struck, having enjoyed the kudos his daughter's marriage brought him, while her mother was never quite so smitten.

Britt's 1964 marriage to Sellers ended 4 years later after many rows and jealousies. They had one daughter, Victoria, 45, a jewellery designer, who had spoken publicly about her unhappy childhood and drug problems. Ekland had alleged that Sellers treated Victoria badly: “No child should receive a letter from their father, telling them not to consider themselves as such," she said in one interview.

However, Britt said there were good times too. "Meeting and marrying Peter Sellers was a mind-blowing experience. Going with him to meet the Queen, being at Windsor Castle, meeting Princess Margaret and Lord Snowdon and going shooting with them, was all an experience." Later on came affairs with a string of famous men including Warren Beatty and Ryan O'Neal and record producer Lou Adler, with whom she had a son, Nikolai, in 1973.

When Ekland and Lou split in 1975, Elizabeth Taylor introduced her to Rod Stewart to cheer her up. "Meeting Rod Stewart and falling in love, so madly in love, was amazing. We were madly in love, we were absolutely obsessed with each other." The rocker, who later left her, was the polar opposite of Sellers, she said. "None of the men I've been in love with, or had a relationship with, have been similar in any way. The only similarity is they have been motivated and very successful at what they do. I've never been drawn by great classical looks, although I thought they looked good," she laughed

Britt remembered the 1960s and '70s as a time of hard work and excitement. She made movies including The Man With The Golden Gun and The Wicker Man, having met everyone from Steve McQueen to Sofia Loren, Cary Grant to the Bay City Rollers. "The only one I didn't meet was Brigitte Bardot, who people used to say I looked like," she said.

In 1984, at the age of 42, Ekland married 23-year-old rock musician Slim Jim Phantom of the Stray Cats, having a son, Thomas Jefferson, 4 years later, before breaking up. She cautioned her own children not to rush into marriage but was delighted when Nikolai, 37, tied the knot two years earlier. "He took his girlfriend to Paris to get engaged. She thought he was taking her to Aspen to see his father but they flew to Britain then took the Eurostar to Paris," she said.

Britt was appearing in Grumpy Old Women at the time, having gone to pick them up from the station when they returned. "Nikolai said, 'We've got something to tell you'. I said, 'How did you know what ring to buy?' He replied, 'From being around you'. She's the most beautiful daughter-in-law. She works with autistic children and is beautiful and natural." Nikolai ran The Roxy on Sunset Strip and her youngest son was a drummer in the band Nylon Pink, but they largely avoided the celebrity magazine circuit.

Ekland was unimpressed with the antics of many of the latest 'stars'. "It's really bizarre, when I was married to Peter Sellers we had no security guards. It was just him and me and his chauffeur who drove us. We had nothing else. With Rod and Jim we had roadies and managers but no security. I don't think the paranoia today is necessary but a lot of stars in any profession want to create hysteria around themselves."

Britt thought celebrities could do more to look good. "Today people don't make the effort. They make a movie and go on tour with designer dresses they borrow to promote it, then the next you see is a picture of them in flip-flops in Starbucks. That's sad, because you lose your fans' love then people see you in the pages of gossip magazines but someone like Victoria Beckham has taken celebrity status to a place it should not be." It was the first vaguely catty thing Ekland had said, despite dropping famous names at every turn.

What did she think of younger celebrities like Katie Price? "I think cosmetic surgery is terrific," Britt said with real passion. "I've had bits and pieces done. I had very outstanding ears and had them pinned back in my 40s. Cosmetic surgery is a very personal thing, it's almost like talking about your underwear. Too many young people think you have to have it but at my age you really have the right to go out and pull your skin up."

Ekland was quite happy to laugh at herself 'pulling her skin up' but, perhaps as a mother, she was genuinely concerned that the young shouldn't be lured into surgery. "When you're 35 I think it's tragic. It's tragic young women have Botox or enormous breasts put on. We didn't have that when I was young. The most revolutionary thing that came out was collagen, when was in my 30s. They put collagen around your mouth or between your eyebrows. We thought it was unbelievable. Sometimes you ended up with a little sausage of collagen but your body soon ate it up!" she giggled.

Britt also power walked and lifted weights to stay fit and travel to where the work was. Her children lived in LA and she had homes in Sweden and London. In Britain Ekland was patron of the Alzheimer's Society, which approached her after her mother died from the disease at 78, who got the disease horribly young in her late 50s.

"She wasn't diagnosed until her mid 60s then she was incarcerated in a hospital for 11 years. She was a little strange for years but nothing was known about Alzheimer's. I was 39 when she died, very young from that point of view and she never saw my younger son, because he was born when I was 46.

I don't think we treat older people as well as we could. If I had to dedicate my life to one thing, it would be to the old and young. These categories of people need help. Children all the way through to pre-teen and up to 18 need a lot of guidance and so do old people. I'll be 68 in October and I'm so grateful that I power walk and lift weights and my brain works. I see people in my age group who can't do this. I wish I could tell everyone to eat right and exercise, so they'll have a fantastic old age, but at the same time, a lot of people don't have the money to do that. It's tragic."

When she wasn't working or doing charity work, Britt liked spending time with her children, who she said stopped her going mad during bad times. "I love being a mother and I think I'm a good mother. I've given my children freedom and manners and a certain moral aspect to life. I think we should give children values and freedom, not the freedom to kill themselves, but enough. I think my children are clever and independent and they've given me enormous comfort in life. I would have gone totally mad if I hadn't had children. I don't know why. I'm just that kind of person."

Ekland had a slight old codger moment when her younger son, Thomas Jefferson, 22, had got a tattoo recently. "He's so cute. He just did his first tattoo." His father had tattoos, so I'm used to them but he's still my little boy, so I was a bit squeamish but, it's fine." Did she have a tattoo? For the first time Britt got a bit coy. "I have a tattoo, it's a rose. Without being too intimate, it's below the waist."

Lightning Source UK Ltd.
Milton Keynes UK
UKHW05f0755230618
324603UK00001B/10/P